MICHAEL ROSEN

CENTRALLY

HEATED
KNICKERS

Illustrated by Harry Horse

PUFFIN POETRY

PUFFIN BOOKS

UK | USA | Canada | Ireland | Australia
India | New Zealand | South Africa

Puffin Books is part of the Penguin Random House group of companies
whose addresses can be found at global.penguinrandomhouse.com.

www.penguin.co.uk
www.puffin.co.uk
www.ladybird.co.uk

Penguin
Random House
UK

First published 2000
This edition published 2017

001

Text copyright © Michael Rosen, 2000
Illustrations copyright © Harry Horse, 2000

The moral right of the author and illustrator has been asserted

Set in 12/14pt Baskerville MT by Jouve (UK), Milton Keynes
Printed in Great Britain by Clays Ltd, St Ives plc

A CIP catalogue record for this book is available from the British Library

ISBN: 978–0–141–38896–0

All correspondence to:
Puffin Books
Penguin Random House Children's
80 Strand, London WC2R 0RL

Contents

1. Environment

2. Design and Innovation

3. Chemistry

4. Physics

star* – Science, Technology and Reading

The star* group is made up of the Royal Society of Chemistry, Institute of Physics, Esso UK and the Design Council, with involvement from Educational Communications. The group asked Michael Rosen to write 100 poems about chemistry, physics, the environment and design and technology. The result is *Centrally Heated Knickers*, a sparkling combination of science and poetry.

1. Environment

1. Engine Oil

My dad said to his friend
'I can't find my funnel.
Can I borrow yours?'
'Funnel?
What d'you need a funnel for?'
'For the oil.
To put the oil in the car.'
'You don't need a funnel for that.
I'll show you.'

He grabbed a plastic bottle
and cut the bottom off it.

'There's your funnel.'

My dad
put the open top of the bottle
down into the hole
for the oil
and the thick yellow syrup
globbed and glooped
through the bottle
into the engine
like it knew the way there
from long ago.

2. Lubricate the Joints

Lubricate the joints
and the railtrack points
the gears
and the shears
and the clocks
and the locks;
the drills
and the mills
and the trimmers
and the strimmers
and the rotors
and the motors
keep them whirring
keep them purring
keep them smooth
on the move
in the grooooooooooooove
oh yeah!

3. Growing Apples

And the King said,
'How do I turn this apple
into thousands of apples?'

The wise men scratched their heads,
muttered amongst themselves
and consulted their great books.

One stepped forward.
'Perhaps this is some kind of joke,
your majesty,
but could one say
that one could make
a thousand apples
by chopping one apple into a thousand pieces?'

'Balderdash!' said the King
'I said thousands of apples
not some nonsensical business
about hacking an apple to bits.'

Another wise man stepped forward.
'I have heard that beyond the horizon
there lives a man
who sings to the objects in his house
it is said of him
that he can cause things to multiply.
Maybe –'

'Poppycock!' roared the King,
'I wasn't looking for some holy-moly jiggery-pokery.'

And on it went.

None of the wise men
were wise enough to solve the problem.

A serving-girl
who was pouring the wine
caught the drift of what was going on.

'I know how to turn your apple
into thousands of apples,' she said.

How the wise men laughed!
'The cheek!'
'A little whipper-snapper like her!'
'As if she'd know!'

'Come then,' said the King,
'Speak, girl!'

'I would bury your apple.'
Said the girl.

There was silence.

The wise men looked at each other
and sniggered.
'Bury it? Bury it?
What good would that do?'

But the King didn't wait.
'You're right, young lady.
Completely and utterly right.'

4. How Humans Out-died

When the Martians landed
in the world they'd been handed
there were no humans left.

They said, 'Do know we how
humans did how out-die?
Mystery is it? Or why?'

One clever young Martian
stepped forward:

'I how know
that humans out-died:
much car
much carbon
much carbon-dioxide.
Exhausted by exhaust;
they car-bon diox-died.'

At that,
another clever young Martian
stepped forward and said:

'Oh no!
Not so!
No oh!

No more rain it was.
That was a pain it was.
That was a strain it was.

So,
it was not so
that humans *died* out.
What it was,
was that
humans *dried* out.'

But then a third clever young Martian
stepped forward and said:

'Humans had old song and sad
and how they sang is this:
'Whatta loada rubbish!
Whatta loada rubbish!

How right were humans
to sing this song so sad
How right were humans
to feel so bad.

For,
rubbish they made
more and more
till the world it filled
from shore to shore.

And that's how
can I tell
was in the world
a terrible smell.

It stank and stank so much,
I thinked
they in the end
became ex-stinked.'

And the Martians all said:

'How right that sounds,
now know we the history
how humans out-died.
Now solved is the mystery.'

5. Wind Force

I stand in the street,
the wind-force
pushes me like a pillow pressed
on my chest.

That's not my brother
doing that
or a machine –
just air
whole housefuls of air
hurling.

If I could grab gusts
of that stuff
I could wreck rockets
ruin roundabouts
or
wrestle with rocks.

But then –
with all that power
perhaps I could
push and pull
enough
to light lights
or make
chocolate biscuits
(the crumbly kind).

6. I Would Die Without

One man said
I would die
without TV

and the other said
I would die
without food.

7. Cold Tomorrow

It was a cold day tomorrow
when we discovered
there was no more wood
no more coal
no more oil
and no more gas
Tomorrow was a cold day.

8. Footsteps

Trot, tread,
trudge, traipse and tramp;
stagger, step,
scamper, stump and stamp;

Hike, skip,
jog, march and amble;
stroll, strut,
shuffle, stride and ramble;

Saunter, lope,
dawdle, plod and toddle;
potter, run,
wander, walk and waddle.

There are many ways
of moving along on foot
and just as many ways
the matter can be put.

9. Acorn, Conker and Key

Hey Acorn!
Who d'you think you are?
A hard guy?
You look like a little hard-boiled egg
sitting in a cup.
Well I'm telling you,
hard guy,
a squirrel is going to find you,
and if he doesn't eat you
he's going to bury you.

Just because you're the start-out point
for the tree
that made the first ships
to go right round the world
doesn't mean you're a big shot.
You're no circumnavigator!

And you, Conker!
Always up for a fight, aren't you?
'Let me get at 'im
Let me get at 'im' –
that's you!
Well, I know your little secret:
there you are,
lying about in your little green house
and then, when the walls split,
out you pop
like you think
you're some shiny new car
cruising out of the garage.

But I've seen inside
your little green house:
you lie for weeks
all tucked up in a soft white bed,
don't you?
Hard man! Huh!

But you, sycamore key,
you're plain weird, plain weird.
You jive about in the air,
jiving in the wind;
cool moves, man!

But then,
you lie on the ground
in a heap
with all the other jivers
looking like a dead moth.
There's hundreds of
you dead moths
lying there.
You're weird.
Where are you *at*?

10. No Sun Day

'I hate you, Sun!
Burning my back
when all I wanted to do
was lie on the beach.
I hate you!'
And the Sun said:
'Don't you talk to me
like that, you little shrimp!
After all I do for you!
One day
I won't *be* here.
Then you'll be sorry.'

11. Dirty T-shirt

My clean T-shirt was dirty.

OK. This is how it goes:
First it was dirty.
Then I washed it.
Now it's clean.
So I put it on the washing-line,
and it dries
and now it's dirty.

That's my dirty, clean T-shirt.
Tiny specks of dirt on it.
But why?
Is someone *throwing* the dirt?
Is the wind *blowing* the dirt?

So I think:
I'll spy on my T-shirt.

The next day

I washed it again,
I put it on the washing-line
and I watched . . .

. . . no one threw anything at it
The wind didn't blow . . .

then it rained.
Ah-hah!

I walked over to the T-shirt.
I whip out my magnifying glass.
I study a bit of the T-shirt
where the rain has fallen on it.

Ah-hah!

Now I know what to do:
Don't leave my washing
out in the rain.
It'll get dirty.
And come to think of it,
it won't get dry either.

Ah-hah!

12. Hot Pants

The tumble-dryer
dries socks hot
and hot socks
make my toes warm.

All through winter
when it's wet and cold
our tumble-dryer
rumbles round.

Hot socks
hot shirts
hot skirts
hot pants

All through winter
in the wet and cold
I watch where the pipe
from the dryer ends:

It's where there's a grille,
and through the holes
the dryer breathes out
hot air.

Hot air
hot breaths
hot puffs
hot pants.

13. If You Make a Mess

I go some places
and it goes like this:

'If you make a mess
you have to clear it up yourself.'

I go some places
and it goes like this:

'If you make a mess
someone else'll clear it up.'

And I go some places
and it goes like this:

'If you make a mess,
no one'll clear it up.'

14. Sun Sounds

If we could hear the sun
would it buzz
like a nest of giant bees?
Would it twitter
like a treeful of birds?
Would it fizz
like a streetful of frying pans?
Would it boom
like a skyful of fireworks?
Or
would it roar
like a worldful of ovens?

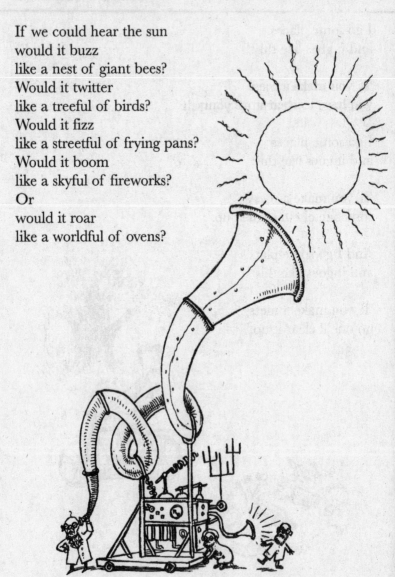

15. Save It

When we're in school
they say to us
we should do all we can
to save energy:
use less electricity, petrol and gas;
use less water.

I don't know why
they keep telling *us*!
They ought to tell
all those people
in the ads for
cars, cookers, petrol, washing machines
and stuff . . .

16. Bypass

All the people in the town said:
we want a bypass.
Send the road
round the town
not right through the middle.
Our children are being
knocked down by the traffic;
people are getting asthma,
the buildings are falling down.

So they built the bypass.

It went through the middle of a wood.
They knocked down trees,
the birds and animals have gone
and the cars and lorries
go whoosh whoosh whoosh

Though sometimes
they go
whoosh whoosh crash.

17. Blobbo

'We must save
energy.
We must save
the environment.'

'I've invented Blobbo –
the stuff that never wears out.'

'Go away – I'm talking.
We must save energy.
We must save the environment.
We must –'

'Blobbo will save energy.
Blobbo will save the environment.
There'll be no need anymore
to have dirty places using up
energy to make things that
keep wearing out.'

'Go away.
No one will make Blobbo.'
'Why not?'
'People will buy it.'
'That's good.'
'That's bad.
People will buy Blobbo,
but then it won't wear out
and then they won't need
to buy any more Blobbo.'

'That's good.
People will save money
and be better off.'

'But all the people making
the stuff that wears out
will be out of a job.'

'But all the people
who've got Blobbo
will have what they want,
they'll be saving money
saving energy
and saving the environment.'

'Go away.
Now –
what was I saying?
Oh yes
We must save energy
we must save the environment,
we must . . .'

18. By Mashed Potato

Wajid said: 'I go to school by bus.'
Linton said: 'I go to school by car.'
Maria said: 'I go to school by train.'
I said: 'I go to school by mashed potato.'

The teacher said: 'Do try to be sensible.
How do you get to school?'
I said: 'By mashed potato.
I eat mashed potato
I turn the mashed potato
into stuff my muscles need.
My muscles make my legs bend.
This makes the pedals on
my bike go round.
I go to school by mashed potato.'

The teacher said, 'Can we say
you come to school
by mashed potato *and*
by bike?'

And I said,
'OK.'

19. Old Bag

This polythene bag
will last as long
as the mummies
in the pyramids.

Hmmm.
Does this mean
that in thousands of years time
people will queue up
to visit the polythene bags?

20. Electricity

I went back to our old flat,
and they were pulling it down.
It was going to be demolished.
My old bedroom was disappearing.
It would be gone forever.

I went up to the builders and
said could I look inside?
I went inside
and there was my bedroom
half-demolished.

I thought
I must take one thing,
one thing to remember it by,
something I looked at a lot . . .
something I touched, perhaps?
Something I touched every day?

Yes, I know –
the light switch.
Perfect.

One of the men broke it off the wall
and gave it to me.
My old light switch.
I keep it on the mantelpiece
in my bedroom
in the new place.

21. The News Today

Today
on the News
they said
there are forty-two million sheep
in this country
and some of them
might have Mad Cow Disease.
If they have got it, they said
then forty-two million sheep
would have to be killed.

Then someone came on and said
the sheep didn't have
Mad Cow Disease
and none of the forty-two million sheep
would be killed.

This was the News today.

22. Yellow Rock

On holiday
on an island in Italy
we saw an old volcano.

We climbed up the side of it
and I picked up
a bit of yellow rock
and put it in my shirt pocket.

By the time
we got back
the stone
had made a hole in my pocket.

sulphur crystals + water + air + warmth → sulphuric acid

23. Giants: a Riddle

As we drew near
we could hear
the thudding
of their hearts
beating.

The moment
we appeared
they stood to attention:
row upon row
across the hillside,
their great white arms
revolving.

It was obvious.
They were communicating
with each other
before making their next move.

It will be
fascinating
to see how they
manage to walk
down the hill
on one leg.

24. Invention

Now that they have
invented
the nuclear bomb
could they please
un-invent it?

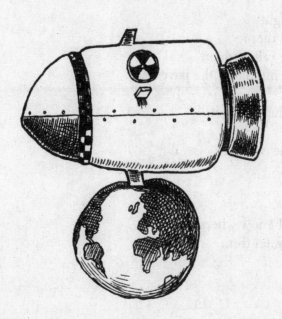

25. Yellow Door

I've often wondered
where gas comes from.

Now I know.

I was walking down the street
and I looked down
at the pavement
and I saw
a little yellow door.

I thought:
why is there
a little yellow door
in the middle of the pavement?

And then I saw it.

On the door
it said:
'GAS'.

Now I know where
gas comes from.

2. Design and Innovation

1. A Speck of Dust

I am a speck of dust.
You must not trust
a speck of dust.

I can fly
in the sky
and land in your eye.

And I have even attacked
a contact lens.

If a contact lens
wearer has time to think,
my fun ends
in a blink.

2. Crossing the Channel

Dad said:

'My plan'll
get us across the Channel.

Instead of crossing over
on the ferry from Dover

the best way on offer
is to go by Hover.'

But
what a bother!
We missed the Hover.

So I said:

'The fun'll
be to go through the tunnel.'

3. Centrally Heated Knickers

I know a man who collects stickers,
like: 'I am wearing centrally heated knickers.'

If it's true, and he's not a liar
I might see him some time with his pants on fire.

4. Duvet Cover

Have you ever tried to shove a
feather duvet in its cover?

My brother bet
I couldn't get
the duvet in its cover.

I thought I could
I said I would.
I tried
but the duvet seemed too wide
to go in there.
'It's not fair
the duvet's all fluffy.'
I was getting huffy.
No matter how hard I tried to stuff
the duvet in. The space wasn't big enough.
The chunks that got in were all lumpy.
You can't sleep under a duvet that's all bumpy.
I tried to crawl in like a mole
but then I got stuck right in the hole.
My brother was dead pleased, he teased:
'You're no good. You've lost the bet.
You couldn't get
your duvet in its cover.'

When I am grown up I shall invent
a way you can shove a
duvet in its cover.
I shall invent
some kind of tent.

5. Beneath My Feet

I stood in the street
and beneath my feet
I felt the purring
and murmuring
of tubes and pipes.

All the people in the houses, shops and factories
switching on and phoning up
washing away and turning off
buttons, taps, levers, controls

and the pipes and tubes hummed
with the flow and current
purring
and murmuring
beneath my feet
in the street.

6. Thirsty Land

In the plane over the desert
I see the badlands beneath us
wrinkled like old skin.

Ancient river valleys
are now dry brown snakes.

The sun that glares at this
has dried up
every last drop.

Even the rocks begin to say:
'Water, please, water.'

7. Cleaning Up

The electrician's been.
So's the plumber.
We've painted the walls
and sanded the table.
Now all we've got to do
is clean up
the bits of wire
the ends of pipes
the chunks of plaster
the piles of sawdust
the wrappers
the labels
the bits of grit
and the balls of fluff.

Anything bigger than a thumbnail
I pick up with my bare hands.
Then Dad switches on the vacuum cleaner.

This blows the fusebox
which cuts off the electrics
which sets off the burglar alarm.
And the vacuum cleaner doesn't work.

It's very hard to clean up
after the electrician
the plumber
the painter
and the sanding
with a vacuum cleaner
that doesn't work.

8. The Lone Survivor

In the bath I go deep-sea diving
looking for old shipwrecks.
Then I am a submarine
cruising into harbour.
I scuba-dive to watch for sharks.
I am an octopus
wrapping tentacles round the rocks.

Then I am a survivor floating in the sea.
Do you know,
though I'm very good at underwater swimming
in the bath
I find it impossible
to be a floating survivor.
I keep sinking.

'Help! Help!
My ship's gone down.
I am the lone survivor.
I am being swept along by the waves.
I'm sinking.
I'm drowning.
Help! Help!'

Mum comes rushing in.
'Are you all right?'
'Yeah, I'm fine.
My ship's gone down.
I'm the lone survivor.'

And she says: 'I don't care what you are,
do you think you could stop shouting?'

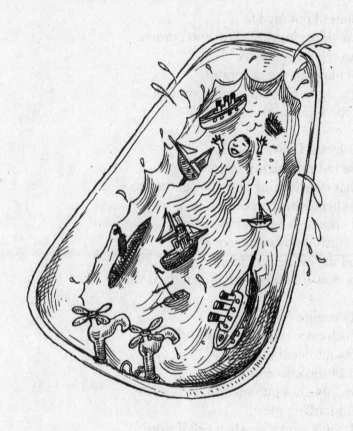

9. Incredible Shrinking Car

I am
The Incredible Shrinking Car.

I started out my life
as a giant chunk of steel and chrome
cruising round town
gobbling up the geography
fighting to find a place big enough
in the supermarket car park.

Bit by bit I have shrunk.
I've lost my mighty bumpers.
That overhanging cliff we call 'my boot'
has been chopped off.
My bonnet's been squeezed
towards the windscreen
and the gate-sized doors
are now no more than little hinged windows.

My engine
which once roared its head off
now mutters to itself
and I slip into corners
like 20p goes into the slot
of a parking meter.
My only worry is: when will it stop?

Will I end up as a
Matchbox toy
on the bedroom floor
of the boy
next door...?

10. Cow Shoes

If a field is boggy
a cow's feet go soggy.
What's more
its feet get sore.

Now here's some news:
they've invented cow shoes.
If you go to a shoe shop now
you might bump into a cow.

11. Scary Sausage-fingers

Hey!
Psst!
I got a trick.
Do you want to know my trick?
I'll tell it to you.
It's called Scary Sausage-fingers.
I'll tell you how you do
Scary Sausage-fingers.

You walk into a room
with Scary Sausage-fingers,
you hold up your hands
and go:
'Look at me! I got
Scary Sausage-fingers!'
and everyone'll go, 'YAAAA!!!'

But first you've got to
make
Scary Sausage-fingers.

You go to the supermarket – without a bag.
You do loads and loads of shopping.
You put it all into the bags
they give you.
You carry it all home.
As you walk along
the handles of the bags
cut into your hands.
It's agony.

But you don't give up.
You walk on home.
The bags still cutting into your hands.
It's double-agony.

You get home.
You drop the bags.
Now you've got
Scary Sausage-fingers.
Big, fat, puffy fingers
with little narrow white bits
in the joints in between
the sausages.

So you rush into where
everyone's sitting quietly
having a nice time
and you hold up your hands
in the air and shout,
'Look! Scary Sausage-fingers!'
and everyone'll go,
'YAAAA!!!'

12. Floating Bridge

The hardest thing about
the first time I went canoeing
was NOT
the strong current on the bend
getting stuck under the trees
losing the paddle
getting tangled in the fishing line
the wave from the powerboat
or
getting bumped by Kenny.

It was the bit where
we stood waiting
to get into the canoes
on a kind of bridge
that floated
and swayed
and bobbed
and lurched
and you could look down
between the planks
and see the dark water
waiting for you to fall in
especially when
Kenny
jumped.

That was the hardest thing
about the first time I went canoeing.

13. Bugs

When people tell me
there's bugs in rugs
there's bugs in jugs
there's bugs in plugs
there's bugs in mugs
and there's bugs in slugs

I just shrugs.

14. Building Blocks

My little sister
makes towers with her blocks.
'Higher,' she says,
'Higher.'
And higher and higher we go
one block at a time
until she shouts,
'Down!'
and hits the tower,
it all falls down
and she rolls over with the blocks
laughing and singing,
'Down! Down! Down!'

But once we had two towers
and she had this idea
we could make a bridge between them.
She kept holding a block
in the gap
between the two towers,
but it kept dropping to the floor.
It wouldn't stay up.
'Up!' she shouted at me.
'I can't,' I said.
'Make it! Make it!'
'It won't stay up on its own,' I said,
and she rolled over on the floor
crying and shouting,
'Up! Up! Up!'

15. Grey Eyes

My dad has brown eyes
My mum has grey eyes
My brother has grey eyes
I have grey eyes

We all sit round the table
and my dad says,
'It's not fair,
you've all ganged up on me.
Six grey eyes
staring at me.'

And I say
'If you had another kid
would his or her eyes be grey?'

And my dad says
'Probably.'

'How do you know?' I say.

'Because the baby that died
had grey eyes too,' he says

16. Boogy Woogy Buggy

I glide as I ride
in my boogy woogy buggy
take the corners wide
just see me drive
I'm an easy speedy baby
doing the baby buggy jive.

I'm in and out the shops
I'm the one that never stops
I'm the one that feels
the beat of the wheels
all that air
in my hair
I streak down the street
between the feet that I meet.

No one can catch
my boogy woogy buggy
no one's got the pace
I rule this place.

I'm a baby who knows
I'm a baby who goes, baby, *goes*.

17. Sharing Pencils

'I think Sean fancies Davina.'
'You must be mad!'
'No, he does.'
'What makes you so sure?'
'You see that pencil he's got?'
'Yeah.'
'It's hers.'
'But that doesn't mean he fancies her.'
'Yeah, but she gave it to him.'
'But that still doesn't mean he fancies her.'
'Yeah, but he's been chewing it.'
'But that doesn't mean he fancies her either.'
'Yeah, but she was chewing it
only a moment before.'
'Oh!'

18. Water Tunnel

In the Waterworld slide
diving down the waterfall tube
rushing along the water tunnel
heading down towards the pool
slipping faster and faster

I suddenly thought
I am an egg
in a snake
I'm an egg
the snake is going to lay

and I skidded
out the bottom of the tube
into the pool,
splosh!

And I thought,
lucky there was water there
otherwise I might have cracked.

Later, when no one's looking,
I will hatch.

19. My Supermarket Queue

When I go shopping at the
supermarket
I have a special queue of my own.

It's the one where
the man in front
has had a massive pile of stuff
all checked out
and he's packed all his bags
and he's discovered he hasn't got enough money.
So he starts taking out stuff
he doesn't think he needs
and he holds it up
one by one
and he says,
'How much is this?'
and he's trying to work out
what he can leave
and it all takes hours
in my own special queue.

It's the one where
the woman in front
bought an avocado
and it's lost its price tag
and avocados don't have barcodes
and the checkout guy
doesn't know the price
and the supervisor
doesn't know the price

and when she goes off
to find the price
the price tag has
fallen off there too
and it all takes hours
in my own special queue.

And it's the one where
the bag of onions splits
a barcode doesn't beep
the till roll jams
the conveyor belt stops
the trainee presses CANCEL
and has to start all over again
while a baby screams
like an aeroplane
because his brother
nicked his biscuit

and it all happens
in my own special queue
and
it
takes

hours!

20. Darren's Car

Now children
today we're going to
use our imaginations
and I want you to think
if you could
turn into an animal
what animal would you choose to be?

Yes, Donna?
A cat. That's nice.
And why would you like to be like a cat?
Because you'd like to be all cuddly
and sit by the radiator in winter
and stay warm.
Lovely.

Darren?
No, Darren. A car isn't an animal.
I'll come back to you in a minute.
Zoe?
A cat. Yes, that's nice,
but let's think of some other animals,
shall we? Yes, Zoe, I understand
you want to be a cat too,
but Donna's the cat.
Yes, I know there could be two cats here,
but Donna used up all the magic that makes cats
you're going to be something else.
You don't want to be anything else.
A leopard? A panther? No?

OK, Zoe, you're a cat.
Just remember you had your chance
to be something else.
Never mind.

Darren!
I've told you
you can't be a car.
No not even your dad's car.
It's just not going to happen for you today!
OK?

Oh, Zoe, now you *do* want to be something else.
What do you want to be?
A jellyfish.
Very interesting.

Mervyn? How about you?
A slug.
Mervyn. Is this all getting . . .
. . . silly?
No?
You want to be a slug
so you can lie about
in your back yard
so that your cousin
will tread on you
and go, 'YEEURCH!!!'
Hmm. Nice, Mervyn. Very nice.

Darren. No. I mean no.
Not your uncle's car
I don't care that your uncle's
got a BMW.
You are not going to be a BMW today.

And Louise?
What would you like to be?
An eagle? A dolphin?
Anyone thought of being
a dolphin leaping through the –
What?
A cockroach.
Louise, why in heaven's name
do you want to be a cockroach?
Oh.
I see.
Because you've got cockroaches
at home
and your mother says
there's nothing you can do
to get rid of them.
Yes, Louise, I get the point,
but cockroaches are – well, er –
OK.
Be a cockroach.

But Darren
You cannot be a car.
You can't be your dad's car.
You can't be your uncle's car
or any car whatsoever.

Er –
well –
Yes.
I understand.
OK. You can be a car
with your dog in it.
Very clever.

Yes, your uncle's BMW
if you like.
No you won't be
doing a ton
on the motorway, Darren.
You've got a dog on board,
Remember?

Well, that starts us off.
We'll do some more of that tomorrow.
Perhaps.

21. Grandad's Chair

I wish
the light wasn't so high up
I wish
the light bulb hadn't blown
I wish
I had been there to change it
I wish
Grandad had used the ladder
I wish
he hadn't used the chair
I wish
the chair had been stronger.

22. Night Rides

... and when the house
is quiet
and everyone sleeps
sometimes I wake up
and breathe in darkness
for so long
I have to get up
open the curtains
and look out over the city
watching the cars do U-turns
that they don't dare do
in the day,
a cat talking to a bin
and a bus full of lovers
sailing down the High Street
lit up like a fairground.

. . . and I think of my big sister
far away
and I want to ride that bus
all the way
up to her block of flats
up the stairs
and in through her door.

The city winks.
I'm cold
. . . and the bus sails on.

23. Bag Words

Today we are learning about bags.

If a paper bag is made of paper
is a handbag made of hands?
is a sandbag made of sand?

An air bag is full of air
so I suppose a plastic bag
is full of plastic.

A carrier bag carries,
so a sick bag is sick.

I know what mailbags
look like
but what do bags of fun
look like?
And can you pack the bags
under your eyes?

I know who let the cat
out of the bag
but who put it in?
I just hope there aren't any cats
in the bags under your eyes!

I've heard there's a
bag of nerves
and a
bag of bones.
Why not put them
in together
with some blood, muscles and skin
and you could have
a bag of person?

All this I understand
But why do people
keep saying
'It's in the bag'?

What's in the bag?
The cat?
The sick?

And while I think about it
which bag is 'it' in?
One of those bags of fun, perhaps?

Shouldn't they say
what they mean
and instead of saying
'It's in the bag'
couldn't they say
what they are talking about
like
'The hand is in the handbag'
or
'The cat is in the bag of nerves'

And then we'd all know
what they're talking about.

24. Drizzy Fink

Hail! Hail!
I come from another
galaxy.
I have been learning English.
I find some of your words
very hard to say.
I will now try to talk
about your fizzy drinks.
I like your fizzy drinks.
I think I will drink
lots of fizzy drinks
and collect
lots of bottles
and lots of tottle bops
    er
    bopple tots
    topple stobs
    pobble lots
    no
    stottle pobs
    tobble spots
    lottle slobs
    lobble slops

Please
can you help me with this?
And please
can I have a drizzy fink?

25. Mum's Dead Coat

A sad thing happened
this week.

It was my mum's coat.

On the label
it says
'The coat that breathes.'

When everyone was out
I went up to it
where it was hanging up
and I put my ear
right close up to it –

but it had stopped breathing!

I don't think mum
has noticed yet.
And I don't know how
to break the news to her.
If I go up to her and say
'Mum, your coat's dead'
I think she'd be upset.

3. Chemistry

1. Straining

Dad was straining the potatoes
when he said to me:
Ssssh!
Don't tell anyone:
some of the spuds have fallen out of the colander
and into the sink.
I've put the ones that fell out
back in with the others.
No one'll notice.
Sssh!
Don't tell anyone.

So I didn't tell anyone.
And he was right.
No one noticed.
No one at all.
He got away with it.
Brilliant.

One problem:
my potatoes
tasted of washing up.

Thanks, Dad.

2. Can You Feel It?

At the club
we had a competition:
who could do the scariest trick.
We did Squidgy Eyeball.
This is how you do Squidgy Eyeball.

First cut a tomato in half . . .
Then you blindfold a victim.
You tell him he's going
to meet someone very special:
Lord Loophole.
You sit the victim down in front
of the guy playing Lord Loophole.

You take the victim's hand,
you make him point his first finger
and you take that finger to Lord Loophole's knee
and you say,

'This is Lord Loophole's knee.
Can you feel his expensive trousers?'

And then you move his finger to Lord Loophole's hand
and you say
'This is Lord Loophole's hand.
Can you feel his fine skin?'

and on . . .

'This is Lord Loophole's shoulder.
Can you feel his expensive jacket?'
'This is Lord Loophole's neck.
Can you feel his silk tie?'

And all the time you're taking
the victim's finger to the place
and making him feel it.

'This is Lord Loophole's chin.
Can you feel his soft skin?'
'This is Lord Loophole's nose.
Can you feel his aristocratic features?'

And then – tricky bit here:
you pull back the victim's finger,
Lord Loophole leans out of the way,
your assistant holds the cut-open tomato
in the place where Lord Loophole's eye was,
you thrust the victim's finger
into the tomato and say:
'This is Lord Loophole's eye.
Can you feel his squidgy eyeball?'
Your victim will scream and yell,
'What is it? Yeeurch!'

That's how we won the competition.

3. Bottle Bank

The bottle bank
gobbled up my bottle
and the bottle bank
went clank.

That's bad. Look at all the work I do
giving it hundreds of bottles to chew.

And that's not all:
at home,
we've got three bins:
one for bottles,
one for paper
and one for tins.

After all that work
I don't think
a bottle bank
should just say clank.
I think
bottle banks
should say thanks.

4. Grandparents' House

At my grandparents' house
they've got a very old plate
with a gold edge round it
and my grandad says,
it's real gold
that's so thin it's like paper.

At my grandparents' house
they've got a very old picture
made of wood,
and my grandma says
that her grandad made it
by cutting out lots of tiny bits
of different kinds of wood
to make all the colours.

At my grandparents' house
they've got a very old newspaper that tells the story of
    how
when my grandparents
were teenagers
they once rowed out to sea
and nearly drowned
and the paper has gone all brown.

At my grandparents' house
they've just fitted a new kitchen
and it looks like it's made of wood
with all the lines and whirly bits
but really it's plastic.

I love going to my grandparents' house
and looking at all their stuff.

5. Woolly Saucepan?

Could I have
a woolly saucepan
a metal jumper
a glass chair
and a wooden windowpane please?

Er – sorry – I mean
a woolly chair
a glass jumper
a wooden saucepan
and a metal windowpane please?

Er – sorry – I mean
Oh – blow it!
You know what I mean,
don't you?

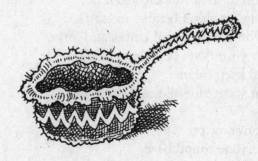

6. Night-time Kitchen

It was all dark in the kitchen
Everyone was in bed,
when suddenly the saucepan said
'It's time I had a bit of respect
around here.
I get thrown about, banged down,
scraped with a spoon,
left for hours covered in old food.
I am made of the finest steel.
I want everyone to know
that if it wasn't for steel
and all the other metals round here
this whole place would
grind to a standstill.

Without us metals, there would be *nothing*.
We are the most important.
They wouldn't be able to cook
without their metal cooker.
They wouldn't be able to eat
without their metal knives and forks.
They wouldn't be able to drink
and keep clean
if it wasn't for all the metal pipes.

From now on
everyone round here
should call us Lord.
Lord Saucepan, Lord Spoon,
Lord Tap and –'

The breadboard had been listening
to all this
and was getting cross.
'Hang on there, Potty!
Those of us round here
who are made of wood
think we've got a case.'
'Huh!' said the saucepan,
'Hark at old Blockhead!'

'No, listen.
Without wooden table and chairs
they'd be eating off the floor.
But without wooden floorboards
they'd be eating off the ground.
But without the wooden beams
the house would fall down
on everyone
so no one would be left alive
to use you, Mr Potty.
If anyone round here ought
to be called Lord
it's people like Floorboard.'

'So,' said the saucepan,
turning to the window,
'who's the most important round here?
Metal or Wood?'

And the window said,
'This is crazy.
We don't think either of you
should boss over the rest of us.
You're both great stuff –
different, but both great.
But watch it –
You, saucepan. They're making
glass saucepans, these days.
And you, table!
Glass tables are really rather fancy.'

And at that
metal and wood
agreed to respect each other
though they're arguing over
which of them
should be the door handle!

7. Where Does the Bounce Come From?

Rubber dubber
flouncer bouncer
up the wall
and in and outer
under over
bouncing backer
mustn't dropper
mustn't stopper
in-betweener
do a clapper
in-betweener
do a spinner
faster faster
to and fro-er
rubber dubber
flouncer bouncer

BUT

then oh bother!
Butter finger
dropped the ball
and pitter patter
patter pitter
rubber ball
ran right away.

8. Sleek Machine: Changes 1

Our car's smooth,
a sleek machine
prowling the street
like a wolf on wheels.

At night it sits
beneath the lamp
its headlights watching
the buses pass.

But in the dark
we know not when
some mean truck
must have backed –
backed up and crashed,
crunched the side
of the sleek machine
in one second flat.

Under cover of the night
it must have revved
and slipped away
leaving our car, a wreck.

The door is twisted
like someone chewed it,
where it was smooth
like a painted egg.

Now it's wrinkled, rucked
like a paper bag
someone screwed up – and chucked.

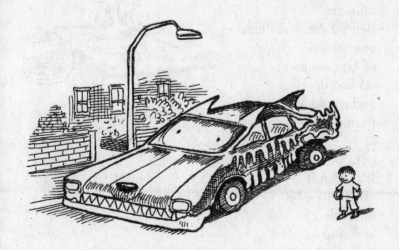

9. Scoop a Gloop: Changes 2

Scoop a gloop
of slimy clay
squeeze it, knead it,
pummel it, stretch it
roly poly, roll it
into long, thin
sausages.
Bend them, coil them
one on top
of one another
up and up
and round and round
to make
a
pot.
It's still soft
and leans a bit
but wait –
and wait –
it slowly hardens
sits dry and dusty
crisp as a biscuit.

Don't tap
or drop
it'll crack
or crumble.
Take it gently
to the kiln
and under fire
of fantastic heat
it strengthens
toughens
enough
to let you
use your spoon
or run your
thumbnail
up and down
your clever coils.

10. Tank Jacket

My dad said
the new tank
in the cupboard
needs a jacket.

I thought
a jacket?
What does it need
a jacket for?
It's not going out.
It hasn't got arms.
It hasn't got anything
to put in pockets.

My dad said,
the new tank
in the cupboard
needs a jacket.

So he went out
and brought it back,
and put it on the tank.

It didn't have sleeves.
It didn't have pockets.
The tank's not going out.

What a waste of money.

11. Simplicity of Electricity

The simplicity
of electricity
is that it never tires
of going down wires.

The invention of plugs
was to stop mugs
who touch wires
becoming electric fires.

The simplicity
of electricity
is that it seems to know
it cannot flow
through plastic.
Fantastic!

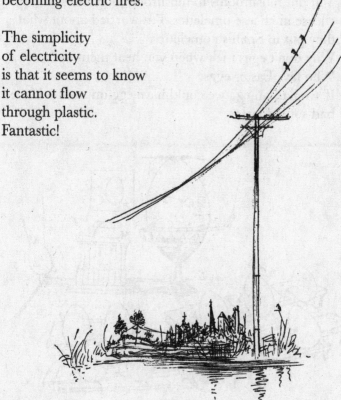

12. Some Thoughts About Eggs: Changes 3

1. Is a hard-boiled egg one that was hard to boil?
2. How fast do runny eggs run?
3. It can't be very fast because my dad beat one.
4. If the white bit's called the 'white', why isn't the yellow bit called the 'yellow'?
5. If a piglet is a little pig, is an omelette a little om?
6. What is an om?
7. You put mushrooms in mushroom omelettes, you put cheese in cheese omelettes. I'm worried about what they put in Spanish omelettes.
8. Why don't eggs melt when you heat them up?
9. Who lays Easter eggs?
10. If we had an egg we could have egg on toast – if we had some toast.

13. Berlam Bam Boola: Changes 4

That night
we made a fire
on the beach
and Alan danced about
singing:
Berlam bam boola
Berlam bam boola
tooty fruity.

I found
a bit of driftwood
that looked like
a cow's skull
and it burned up bright
Berlam bam boola
berlam bam boola
tooty fruity.

When we found
the remains of the fire,
in the ashes
I could just make out
the shape of a cow's skull.

14. Pouring

Whether it's hot,
or whether it's not
I don't see how
you pour a teapot.

I can see
you *can* pour tea,
but you surely cannot
pour a teapot.

15. Chippy Breath

After football
my dad buys me fish and chips
and my hot chippy breath
makes clouds in the air
and rain on the windows
of the bus
all the way home.

I write the score
on the wet glass
– but only when we win.

16. Button Box – Sorted!

I go fishing
in the button box
digging my hand
deep down inside,
making a cup
with my fingers,
pulling my hand
slowly upwards,
letting the small boring buttons
slip through the gaps
between my fingers . . .

. . . so I can catch
the gold buckle
off grandma's shoe,
the fat domed button
that comes dressed
in purple cloth,
the American Army badge,
and the glass eyeball
that stares at me
from the palm of my hand.

17. Making Jelly

It's my job
to take the slab of jelly
and break it up into cubes.

It's mum's job
to pour on the boiling water
to melt the cubes.

It's my job
to stir it up
until there are no lumps left.

It's her job
to put the bowl
in the fridge to help it set.

It's my job
to eat it.

18. Summer Leftovers

The washing machine
rinses the summer holiday away
and when everything's dry
it all goes into
my chest of drawers,
with the clothes
I didn't take.
That's it.

Summer over
till next year.
The beach, the surf,
the sun, the wind,
all washed away.

Weeks later
I am putting on a pair of socks
and there's the summer!
The beach, the surf,
the sun, the wind,
in the sand
caught in the toe of a sock.

19. Salty Wave

When I went through the wave
I gobbled a great gulpful
of saltwater.

That night in bed
my hand nestling on my neck
found tiny crusts; white grains.

And when I licked my fingertip,
it was as salty
as a crisp – or a wave.

20. The Solution

When my sister
is better
she won't have to lie in bed
between two upside-down
water bottles
with tubes going into her.

They must know my sister very well,
because
one's got a little bit of salt in it
while the other's got
quite a lot sugar.

They could have done better
with that sugar one, though:
they should have made it
with chocolate milkshake.

Never mind.
When my sister
is better
she won't have to lie in bed
between two upside-down
water bottles
with tubes going into her,
and I'll make her
a big fat
mega-mega
chocolate milkshake –
KER-PAM !!!

21. How Not to Make Mayonnaise

A French friend of Dad's
was making mayonnaise.
He poured
and mixed
and whisked
for hours
and he kept saying:
It is going to be marvellous,
it is going to be superb.

A woman walked past.

He cried out:
It is destroyed.
It is completely destroyed.

Destroyed? said my dad.
Yes, he said,
the lady with the beard breathed on it.

Later, at home,
Dad said,
I didn't see her breathe on it.
And I said,
I didn't see her beard.

22. Cold Pickles, Warm Chutney and Hot Jam

One year
Mum made
pickled new green cucumbers
and the house smelled
of vinegar and peppercorns
all the way
from the front door
to my bedroom.
Whoever came to the house
went away with
a jar of pickled new green cucumbers.
Even the man who read
the gas meter.

The next year
Mum made
green tomato chutney
and the house smelled
of vinegar and hot tomatoes
all the way
from the front door
to my bedroom.
Whoever came to the house
went away with
a jar of green tomato chutney.
Even the man who painted the windows.

Last year
Mum made gooseberry jam
and the house smelled
of melting sugar and fruit juice
all the way
from the front door
to my bedroom.
Not many of the people
who came to the house
got a chance
to get hold of
a jar of that gooseberry jam.

23. Melting

The butter melted
the cheese went mouldy
it all got so hot
the cat moulted.

The it got hotter
the cheese melted
and the cat went mouldy.

Then it got hotter
and the cat melted.

24. Concrete Paw

Our friends next door
have moved away.
They put everything
in a van today.

They got in a car
and went.
That's it.
No one's left.

My friend's gone.
Her sister's gone.
Their mum's gone.
Their dog Sniffy's gone.

Everyone's gone.
Nothing left . . .

. . . except for
the mark of Sniffy's paw
printed into the concrete
by their front door
where it'll stay
forever more.

25. Some Advice for You If You're Ever Thinking of Walking Across a Very Old Iron Bridge

Don't trust
rust.

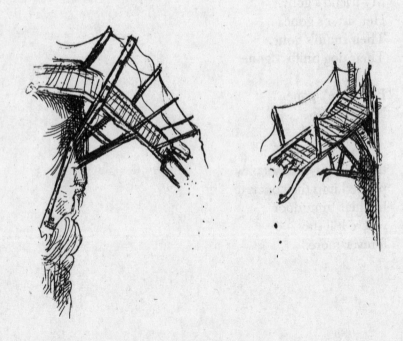

26. Barbecues

When it began to drizzle
I thought the whole thing would fizzle
out.
But there was no need to grizzle
about it, because soon the stuff started to sizzle
and in the end it was
GREAT!

I love it when *we* have barbecues
in the garden, but it really doesn't amuse
me when the next door neighbours use
theirs. I refuse
to believe our one makes as much
smell and smoke as their one –
which I
HATE!

27. Chocolate

Look at me, look at me,
I've got chocolate.
It's the end of the party
they've given me chocolate.
Look at me, look at me
I've got chocolate.
I must keep my chocolate
where no one can get it.
Where shall I put it
in my bag? In my pocket?
No. In my hand, I'll keep it.
Look at me, look at me
I've got chocolate
and I'm going home to eat it.

And we walk down the street,
it's a sunny day and hot
for me and my chocolate
and I've got it, I've got it,
my fingers are round it
tightly closed round it,
look at me look at me
I've got chocolate.

And we get to my house
and I rush in and shout
'Look at me, look at me,
I've got chocolate . . .'
And I open up my hands
to show them the chocolate . . .
. . . and oh no!
What do you know!
That lovely bit
of beautiful chocolate
has gone all soggy
mucky and sticky
like a handful of mud
and all I've got,
is a big sticky mess
oh no, oh yes!
'Look at you, look at you
what are you going to do?'
And I stop and I think
and I think and I stop.
What's in my hand?
What have I really got?
Is it still chocolate?
Is this mess chocolate or not?
I know what
I'll just try a little taste
I take my tongue to my finger
and my finger to my tongue
and YUM!

Look at me, look at me
lick lick lick
chocolate lick
lick it, like it
like it, lick it
sticky, sticky chocolate
lick it and lick it
till there's nothing left
not one little bit.

I've eaten my chocolate.
Look at me.

4 Physics

1. Granma's Hands

My Granma's seventy-two.
She says she's getting old.
My Granma's seventy-two.
She says her hands are cold.

My Granma stands at the bus stop
in all kinds of weather.
My Granma stands at the bus stop
rubbing her hands together.

'I always rub me hands,' she says
'when I'm running from pillar to post.
'I always rub me hands,' she says
'ooh, they're warm as toast.'

2. Floating High-rise

At night
in the harbour
the ships tower above us
like high-rise blocks of flats.

I think
they're great buildings
with kitchens and bedrooms
and a thousand stairs.

Inside
there are car parks full of cars
and the windows are lit up
across and down
and right up to the top
just like office blocks
and city buildings.

All that steel and glass.

Humming in the middle
you can hear the mass of engines
turning and turning.

And if you wait
there comes a moment
when these buildings move.

They shudder
and nudge out
into the harbour.

And you see clearly now
across the water
that this great building
dares to float.

3. Cat's Eyes

I watch
I watch my cat
I watch my cat's eyes

she lies in the sun
blinking
following the butterfly
with the middle of her eye
no more than a pencil line

I watch
I watch my cat
I watch my cat's eyes

she sits in the dark
staring
following a fly
with the middle of her eye
as round and glassy as a big black marble

I watch
I watch my cat
I watch my cat's eyes

4. Wind-up Mouse

You daft, tiny plastic mouse
causing chaos round the house.
Our puppy dogs
hear your cogs
come jumbling through the door
to see you running round the floor.

You crazy, little, wizzy wind-up
whirring round where we are lined up
pointing and shouting
at your fizzing about-ing
until with a twitch and a sideways hop
your little wheels skid to a stop.

You muddle-headed, shiny, pink nutter
you start with a rush and end with a stutter.
We run behind
to get a turn to wind
the little key sticking out of your side
that sends you on another ride.

5. Periscope

The boy
next door
is a bit of a dope.

I'm very clever.
Not like him.
I hope.

Between our houses
there runs a wall.
The wall is tall.
But I am small.

D'you know
this means:
because I'm small . . .

. . . I can't see
over that wall.

There's nothing
that I'd like more
than to look over that wall
at him next door.

P'raps
when I'm older
I'll be tall.

Then I'll be able
to look
over that wall.

Meanwhile . . .

For my birthday
I very much hope
I will get
a periscope.

6. Kaleidoscope

It is said that the Great Emperor of all Emperors
called for his wisest and cleverest people
and told them to go away for ten years
to invent useful things.

Whoever could invent the most useful thing of all
would win 3500 chocolate biscuits.

Ten years later
there was a queue outside the palace
of the Great Emperor of all Emperors.

One by one,
people were asked in
to show their invention
to the Great Emperor of all Emperors.

One woman had invented
windscreen wipers for spectacles.
'Excellent,' said the Great Emperor,
'very useful for when it's raining,
but not a prize-winner, I'm afraid.'

One man had invented
square tomatoes.
'Very good,' said the Great Emperor
'very useful for putting tomatoes in boxes,
but not a prize-winner, I'm afraid.'

One woman had invented
a pencil that sharpened itself.
'I like it,' said the Great Emperor
'Very useful when you're too tired to use a pencil
    sharpener,
but not a prize-winner, I'm afraid.'

And one man had invented
the kaleidoscope.
'What's this?' said the Great Emperor.
'You look through it,' said the man.
'It's a telescope, is it? Well, I'm afraid
telescopes have already been invented.
Hard luck. Goodbye. Next!'

'It's not a telescope,' said the man,
'but you *do* look through it.'
'What's the point of looking through
something that *looks* like a telescope,
but *isn't* a telescope?' said the Great Emperor.

'You look through it,
then you twist it and move it
and before you know what's what
you find yourself saying, 'Ooh!'
Or, on another day,
you might look through it,
twist it and move it
and you could find yourself saying, 'Ahhh!'
And I have to tell you this:
sometimes people find themselves saying both 'Ooh!' *and*
    'Ahhh!''
'But what's the use of that?' said the Great Emperor.
'I asked for inventions that are *useful*
not some stupid little thing that makes
you make funny noises.
Thank you and goodbye. Next!'

'Just try it,' said the man.

'Oh, if I must!' said the Great Emperor crossly.
And he picked up the kaleidoscope.
He twisted it and moved it
and he looked through it.
And when he saw all the colours of the rainbow
glowing in there
and when he saw all those patterns
changing over and over again
he said,
'Ooh!'
And then he said,
'Ahhh!'

Then,
as he went on looking through it
and changing the patterns, he said,
'Yes, it's very nice,
but what's it *for*?
Is it *useful*?'

And the man who had invented the kaleidoscope said,
'If you think about it,
it's *very* useful.
People go all over the world to look for things
like the Grand Canyon
or the Eiffel Tower
so that when they see them they will say,
'Ooh!' and Ahhh!'
With this invention
you won't have to move out of your chair.
All you have to do is carry it in your pocket.
And whenever you feel like a quick 'Ooh!'
or a quick 'Ahhh!'
you take it out,
look through it
twist it about a bit
and there you are . . .'

But the Great Emperor wasn't listening.
He was too busy
looking through the world's first kaleidoscope
and saying, 'Ooh!' and 'Ahhh!'

Later
much later
the man won 3500 chocolate biscuits.

Well,
that's how the story goes.
It may or may not be true.

7. Shadow

Across my bedroom wall
flapping its giant grey wings:
a monster.

Across my bedroom lamp
fluttering its small brown wings:
a moth.

8. He Pulled, We Pushed

It wasn't my fault
the sofa got stuck in the door.

You see, my dad said
it had come in through the door
so it was obvious
it had to be able to get out the same way.

So he was up one end
and my sister and me were up the other
and we headed for the door.

It looked like it would go through
on its side
kind of leaning over.
He pulled.
We pushed.
But it wouldn't go.

Then it looked like it would go through
standing up
kind of twisted round.
We pulled.
He pushed.
But it wouldn't go.

Then it looked like it would go through
upside down
kind of legs first.
He pulled.
We pushed . . .

. . . and it really was looking good
it was halfway through that doorway
when my dad said,
'What's it look like your end?'

And it looked good.
Really it did.
So I said,
'OK.'

Why did I say
'OK'?

If I could have my time over again
the one thing
I would NOT say, is
'OK.'
But I did.

So he pulled.
And we pushed.
And – KER-unfffff.
It stuck.
In the doorway.
The doorway of the front door.

Where everyone comes in
and everyone goes out.

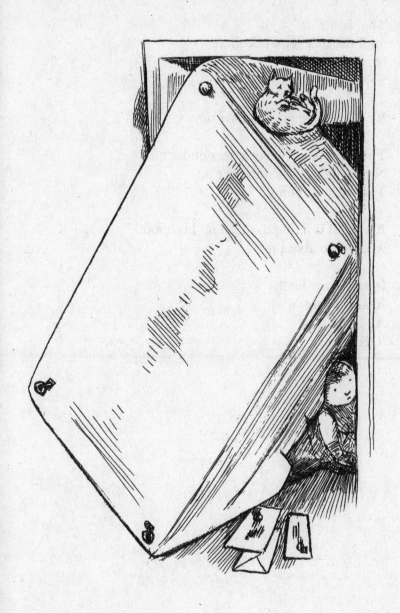

That is
until the sofa got stuck there
because I said,
'OK.'

It's been there for two days now.

The postman delivers letters under it.
Next door's kids climb over it.
The cat sleeps on it.

And Dad is trying to make up his mind
what to do about it.

It wasn't my fault.
Really it wasn't.
All I said was
'OK.'

9. Jumping Jack

To make my little brother giggle
all I have to do is wriggle.

The game he wants me most to play
is one where I look cross and say:

'Get back in your box
Jack-in-a-box
and don't come out till I tell you.
Do what I say
or come what may
I'm afraid I will have to sell you.'

So Jack-in-a-box
goes back in his box
and I say, 'He'll never come out.'
Then the lid flies back
up jumps Jack
and I look shocked and shout.

And my little brother
laughs and laughs
till you think he's had enough.
Then he looks at Jack
and says to me
'More of that Jumping Jack stuff!'

10. High and Low Song

Once I was in a show at school
and we had to sing a song
about a man that likes to go wandering in the mountains;
We sang:
'I love to go a wandering
along the mountain track . . .'

Every day we practise.
And the song goes very high.
And the song goes very low:

'. . . I love to go a wandering
with my knapsack on my back.'

Every day we practise
and it's getting more and more boring.

                          eee

                    ree

'. . . val de

                    ah

          rah

val de
with my knapsack

         on

                my

                    back.'

Every day we practise
and we all have to sing exactly together.

We all have to sing the word 'back'
at exactly the same time
very quickly:
'back!'
and it's all getting tremendously boring
so one day we are singing it over and over again
and we all went high on the high bit
and we all went low on the low bit
and we all sang exactly together – 'back!'

And in the little gap
after 'back!'
I called out, 'Jack'.

                    eee
            ree
'val de'
                    ah
        rah
val de
with my knapsack
        on
                my
                back!'
                    'JACK!'

And everybody laughed.
And everybody thought it was funny.
And I was thrown out of the show.

11. Christmas Tree Lights

My dad is the world expert on
Christmas tree lights.
No one is allowed to touch the
Christmas tree lights
He goes up to the attic
he finds the box of
Christmas tree lights
He brings it downstairs
and takes out the
Christmas tree lights
He walks round the tree
draping it with
Christmas tree lights
He rubs his hands
and wipes his nose and
switches on the
Christmas tree lights
and every year
it's always the same
one of the bulbs has blown on the
Christmas tree lights

He rants and raves
and waves his arms
and curses the
Christmas tree lights
And every year
it's always the same
it's us, not him,
who has to go to the shops
and hunt for spare bulbs for the
Christmas tree lights.

12. Elastic

No one laughed.

For days
we had been winding elastic bands
round our fingers
to make catapults

For days
we had been folding paper
into different shapes
to make pellets

For days
we had been pulling back the elastic
to fire off at each other

This time
no one laughed

Wendy Sutton opened the window
Jeff Clarke fired the pellet
The pellet hit Wendy Sutton
Wendy Sutton lost the sight in her right eye

We stopped making elastic band catapults.

13. Grandad's Airer

My grandad says
when he was a boy
he lived in a flat
and in winter
when they wanted to dry the washing
they used an 'airer'.

It was like a clothes horse
lying on its side
that they hoisted up to the ceiling
with a rope and pulley.

The trouble was, he said,
it was next to the cooker.

Just where
they fried liver and onions.

So when he stood in line at school
the kids behind would sniff his shirt
and point and say:
'Liver and onions!'

14. The Sun and the Moon

Some people say
nothing's ever simply black and white
nothing's ever simply this or that
they say the truth lies somewhere in-between.

That's OK
but I read how years ago
some people said the sun goes round the earth
and they tried to kill the people
who said the earth goes round the sun.

I've figured out
in the case of this earth-and-sun thing
the truth does not lie somewhere in-between.

15. What's the Time, Keith?

So that he can tell
if it's time for his favourite TV programme
my friend Keith's got a
water-resistant
heat-resistant
shock-resistant
digital watch.

It's been tested
underwater
in an oven
and under a hammer.

It's got a
calendar
a light
a stopwatch
round-the-world times
lap times
chimes
buzzers
and bells.

It's so COOL!

Most of the time he leaves it by his bed
at home.

16. Faster and Faster

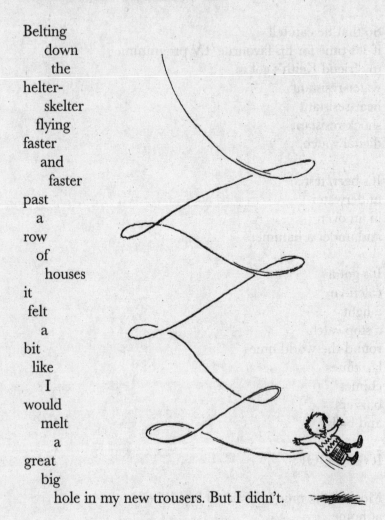

Belting
  down
    the
helter-
  skelter
    flying
faster
  and
    faster
past
  a
 row
  of
   houses
it
 felt
  a
bit
 like
  I
would
  melt
   a
great
  big
    hole in my new trousers. But I didn't.

17. Fridge Magnets

After our holiday in the States
we came back with fridge magnets:
a tiny bubble gum dispenser that rattles
a juke box that plays Rock Around the Clock
an English telephone box that rings
an American payphone that rings
a kitchen blender that whirrs
a knickerbocker glory
and
a poem.

When my sister comes in
she rattles the tiny bubble gum dispenser
she plays Rock Around the Clock
she rings the English telephone box
she rings the American payphone
she whirrs the blender
she licks the knickerbocker glory
and she reads
the poem.

She takes a drink from the fridge,
slams the door and
the tiny bubble gum dispenser that rattles
the juke box that plays Rock Around the Clock
the English telephone box that rings
the American payphone that rings
the kitchen blender that whirrs
and the knickerbocker glory
drop off the fridge door.

The poem stays there.

18. Keep Warm, Keep Cool

In winter
when we go for walks
we take hot drinks
in flasks
and we bury them deep
in our bags
wrapped up in woolly hats.

In summer
when we go for walks
we take cold drinks
in flasks
and we bury them deep
in our bags
wrapped up in woolly hats.

19. Spoon Faces

'Look at you
in the spoon
you're upside down
your nose is too big
your eyes are too wide
you look like a pig.'

'So?
Look at *you*
in the spoon
you're upside down
your nose is too big
your eyes are too wide
you look like a pig.'

'But you look horrible.'

'So do you.'

'I know. It's great, isn't it?'

20. Steamy Shower

I love a
dreamy, steamy shower
hanging about
for over an hour
just before bed
getting hot and red
in the steam
standing there
with time to dream
water-running-over-me feeling
drips dripping off the ceiling
Mum says it's my fault it's peeling
nothing can beat
the hot wet heat
nothing wetter
nothing better
I love a
dreamy, steamy, streamy shower.

21. It Must Have Dropped into the Street Below

Whenever I do something naughty
my dad says:
'Oh yes. Like the time you threw your mother's best ring
out of the window.
It was her grandmother's.'

I only know I threw my mother's best ring
out of the window
because my dad tells me.
I don't remember doing it.
I was three.

And it was never found again.

We live over a shop
and it must have dropped into the street below.

I sometimes wonder why I did it.
Did I want to see it sail through the air?
Wheeeeeeeeee
Did I want to see it land on the pavement?
Clink, clink, clink
Or was it just to see it flying out of the window?

All I know is:
whenever I do something naughty
like scribble on the wallpaper
or put toothpaste in his shaving soap
my Dad says:
'Oh yes. Like the time you threw your mother's best ring
out of the window.
It was her grandmother's.'

22. Making Rainbows

I've got a friend who says
he can make rainbows
and Keith says:
'Yeah, sure. What do you mean?
Are you saying you can *paint* rainbows?'

'No,' he says,
'I can make rainbows.'
And Keith says,
'Yeah, sure. What do you mean?
Are you saying you *dream* you make rainbows?'

'No,' he says,
'I can make rainbows.'
He took us out into his back yard
and filled a watering can
he looked to see where the sun was coming from
he poured out some water
in a big wide spray.
We looked.
He was right.
There was a rainbow.

'See,' he said,
'I can make rainbows.'

And Keith said,
'That's not a rainbow, is it?
Not a rainbow that goes right across the sky
in the rain.'
And we said,
'Shut up Keith.'

23. Doorstep

The first cold bite
of the winter wind
sinks in
just as you tread
on to the front doorstep
where the cat
has snuggled up
to the front door
to make herself warm

24. Floating Balloon

My balloon from the fair
hangs in the air
nosing the ceiling.
Its string hangs down
like a tail to the floor

I lie in bed
watching it tremble
and it quivers
when I give a blow.

I dream of peaches
that float round trees

But in the morning
my balloon from the fair
squats on the floor
its tail snaking over the carpet

I get out of bed
watching it roll
and it bounces
when I give it a kick.

25. Wood – Cool!

He wouldn't use
a wooden spoon

but a wooden spoon
would do.

With it being so hot
in the cooking pot

a wooden spoon
would keep cool.

Wouldn't you sooner
use a wooden spoon

if you knew
the pot was hot?

Maybe you would.
Maybe not.